AmericanGirl Library™

Games and Giggles

Just for Girls!

Illustrated by
Paul Meisel

PLEASANT COMPANY

First Edition.
Printed in the United States of America.
95 96 97 98 99 KRH 10 9 8 7 6 5 4

American Girl Library™ is a trademark of Pleasant Company.

Editorial Development by Deb Eaton, Jodi Evert,
Patricia Ann Lynch, Stacey Sparks, and Jeanette Wall
Art Direction by Kym Abrams, Marla Brenner, and Jane S. Varda

Library of Congress Cataloging-in-Publication Data

Games and giggles just for girls / illustrated by Paul Meisel. — 1st ed.
p. cm. — (American girl library)
Summary: Includes an assortment of wordsearches, crossword puzzles, and word games,
tricks, mazes, number games, travel games, and more.
ISBN 1-56247-232-1 (pbk.)
1. Games for girls—Juvenile literature. 2. Amusements—Juvenile literature. [1. Games.
2. Amusements.] I. Meisel, Paul, ill.
GV1204.998.G35   1995   790.1'94—dc20   95-10868   CIP   AC

Contents

The Giggle Gang

Game Time!

Those fun-loving girls from the Giggle Gang are playing their favorite games. Study this scene for as long as you like. Turn the page to see how many questions you can answer—without looking back!

★

1

Game Time!

Let's see how much you remember about that picture from page 1:

1. How many girls are in the picture? 10
2. Does the girl jumping rope have long hair or short hair?
3. What board game are the girls playing?
4. One girl is playing hopscotch. What color is her shirt?
5. What color is the puppy, and what is she chasing?
6. How many girls are playing cards?
7. How many jacks are on the ground?

Wacky Wordsearch

Hidden in this puzzle are ten words that have something to do with laughter. The words are backward, forward, diagonal, and up and down!

Word Box

| silly | fun | grin | tickle | gag | chuckle | laugh | joke | knock knock | roll |

```
T  S  F  O  U  E  L  I  M  S  N  F  J  A
V  I  B  N  A  W  O  L  M  P  U  M  I  B
A  L  K  O  J  P  G  R  I  N  R  A  C  D
S  L  G  Q  Z  G  U  O  F  M  H  E  L  D
R  Y  C  T  I  C  K  L  E  A  G  W  Z  D
O  L  E  G  U  P  E  L  K  C  U  H  C  A
V  S  A  L  E  K  O  J  C  N  A  H  O  L
U  G  S  P  A  H  T  H  I  M  L  L  P  I
K  N  O  C  K  K  N  O  C  K  I  S  T  A
```

Tummy Ha-Ha

For this game you need at least three friends who feel like getting really silly. First, set up the "tummy" part of the game. Lie down on the floor. Have another friend lie down with her head resting on your tummy. Have your other friends lie down in the same way, until you've formed a head-to-tummy human chain. Now for the "ha-ha" part. Start the game with a simple "ha." Not a dainty, polite "ha," but a deep-down from the bottom of your belly "HA!" If you've done it well, the head resting on your tummy will bounce. The next person says "HA! HA!," the person after that says, "HA! HA! HA!," and so on. Soon, everyone will catch the giggles!

It's a Fact: When you frown, you use 43 muscles. When you smile, you use only 17.

Games Galore Crossword

The answers to the clues all have something to do with games American girls play.
Look in the word box below for hints!

Across

1. You twirl it.
3. Game with knights and pawns
5. String game
9. Kick the _____
10. In mini-_____, you mostly putt.
12. Heart, diamond, spade, _____
13. Ready, set, _____!
14. Game on ice
15. Freeze or shadow _____
17. Blind _____ _____
20. You do it with a tail.
21. In almost every game, you want to _____.
22. Where you first put your foot in Hokey Pokey
23. _____ _____ seek
24. _____ potato or red _____ pepper

Down

1. You bounce a little ball and try to catch them.
2. _____, may I?
4. You could use one for a blind fold.
6. Game played on a red and black board
7. Game where two ropes are twirled
8. Crazy _____
11. Red _____, green _____
16. _____ rummy
17. Old _____
18. If you cover a row with markers, you yell _____!
19. What you try to do in a treasure hunt
20. "_____ ball!"

Word Box

jump rope	in	chess	hide and	bingo
cats cradle	can	hot	jacks	find
man's bluff	go	mother	scarf	play
checkers	club	tag	golf	maid
double Dutch	pin	eights	light	gin
hockey	win			

Mirror Image

Do you believe a mirror can take pictures the way a camera does? Your friends will, after you wow them with this terrific little trick. You need a hand mirror, a partner, and an unsuspecting audience.

The trick.

You leave the room, and your partner pretends to photograph a volunteer's face using the hand mirror. When she calls you back, you astound everyone by telling them whose picture was taken!

The secret.

Your partner silently lets you know who she photographed by copying how that person is sitting or standing. While your eyes study your audience, your mouth tells a story to distract them: "Hmmm, the picture's a little fuzzy. . . mirror photos take a while to develop . . . kind of like those instant photos . . . maybe if I tap the mirror a little. . . blah, blah, blah." If you're smooth, you'll fool them every time.

Who's Missing?

Play this game with ten or more friends. Pick one girl to be IT, and ask her to leave the room. While she's gone, have another friend hide. Then have IT come back. She has ten seconds to name the girl who's missing!

Appearances Can Be Deceiving

Can you find the seven short words in the word "appearance"?
The letters for each short word are next to each other and in the right order.

APPEARANCE

ERR - PEAR - RAN ★ PEA - AN - APPEAR - A

 Eye Foolers

These questions are trickier than they seem! Use a ruler to check your answers.

1. Is one square bigger than the other?

2. Is one line longer than the other?

3. Look at circles A and B. Is one bigger than the other?

To the Airport!

Candice and her family are late meeting Grandma's plane at the airport. Draw a line to get them from their house to the airport. And step on it!

STOP

DETOUR

ROAD CLOSED

Geography

Geography is a word game for two or more players. **Player 1** says the name of a place—a city or state or country. **Player 2** thinks of the letter that the place ends with and names a place that begins with that letter. **Player 3** continues in the same manner. For example,

 Player 1: New Yor<u>k</u>
 Player 2: <u>K</u>ansa<u>s</u>
 Player 3: <u>S</u>an Francisc<u>o</u>
 Player 1: <u>O</u>rego<u>n</u>
 Player 2: <u>N</u>evad<u>a</u>
 Player 3: <u>A</u>nnapolis

A player is out when she can't think of a place that begins with the right letter. The last player left is the winner.

AG Code 1

The American Girl decoder below shows symbols that represent each letter of the alphabet. Use the decoder to find out the answer to this question: **What does your friend say when you ask her to sleep over?**

⌐ < ⌐ ⌐. > ⌐
<u>A</u> <u>L</u> <u>A</u> <u>S</u> <u>K</u> <u>A</u>

∧ <
<u>M</u> <u>Y</u>

∧ ⊔ ⌐. ⊓ ▢ ▢.
<u>M</u> <u>O</u> <u>T</u> <u>H</u> <u>E</u> <u>R</u>!

Tricky Type

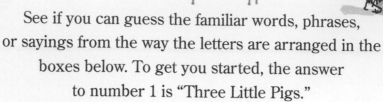

See if you can guess the familiar words, phrases,
or sayings from the way the letters are arranged in the
boxes below. To get you started, the answer
to number 1 is "Three Little Pigs."

1. pigpigpig	**2.** heart	**3.** STUCK ↑
4. WICH PBJ SAND	**5.** Trouble Trouble	**6.** STRIKE STRIKE STRIKE → YOU'RE
7. SHAME YOU	**8.** COW	**9.** LO falling VE

10

10. Joe's Joe's Joe's Joe's Joe's	**11.** Fever	**12.** ME MY
13. THUMB	**14.** history history history history history history history history history	**15.** Comic
16. BAG	**17.** GRACE	**18.** COCO ◯

Be a Mathmagician

It's true. Math can be a little bit magical. Don't believe it? Try these tricks with your friends. They might need paper and a pencil.

1. **You say:** "Think of a number from 1 to 5.

   Double it.

   Add 2.

   Divide by 2.

   Now subtract the number you first thought of.

   When I snap my fingers, we'll both say the answer...

   The answer is 1!"

2. **You say:** "Think of a number.

   Multiply it by 2.

   Add 4.

   Divide by 2.

   Subtract the number you first thought of.

   When I snap my fingers, we'll both say the answer...

   The answer is 2!"

3. **You say:** "Think of a number.

   Add 9.

   Multiply by 2.

   Subtract 4.

   Divide by 2.

   Subtract the number you first thought of.

   When I snap my fingers, we'll both say the answer...

   The answer is 7!"

Magic 15

Put the numbers 1, 3, 4, 6, 7, and 9 in the blank squares below so that all the rows—horizontal, vertical, and diagonal—add up to 15.

8		
	5	
		2

Triangle Tangle

How many triangles can you count in the large triangle at left?

Hidden Numbers

There's a number hiding in each sentence below. When you find it, put a box around it and write the numeral above the box. To get you started, the first one is done for you.

1. At camp we have fu n in every kind of weather.

2. Pat won the road race.

3. Becca swims even whcn the sun isn't shining.

4. I made our neighbor's dog get off our porch.

5. Brittany's height helps her make basket after basket.

6. Both reels for my fishing rod are broken.

7. There was a goldfinch on each perch of the feeder.

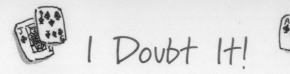

I Doubt It!

The key to winning this card game is pretending, or **bluffing**. If you can look your friends in the eye and tell them you're laying down three 5s when you're actually laying down only two 5s and a king, you're going to be great at this. To play, you need a deck and a half of cards and up to four friends. The goal is to get rid of all your cards. Here's what you do:

1. Shuffle the cards and deal them all face down. Pick up your cards and sort them by number.

2. The player to your left goes first. Let's call her Hannah. She must begin with 2s. As she lays down her 2s in a neat stack, face down, she calls out what she's playing. For example, "Three 2s."

3. Now you and all the other players have a decision to make. Do you believe Hannah, or is she bluffing?

4. If a player thinks Hannah is bluffing, she challenges her by yelling, "I doubt it!" Then Hannah turns her cards face up, and you find out one of two things:

It's the truth. If Hannah *does* have three 2s, the player who doubted her has to take the cards.

It's a bluff. If Hannah laid down three cards and they're not all 2s (or none is!), she has to take them back. The bluff can be even sneakier—Hannah may try to lay down more than three cards. If she's caught, she takes them all back.

5. If no one challenges Hannah, the cards stay face down on the table. The next player who loses a challenge has to take all the cards on the table.

6. The game continues in the same way. The next player lays down 3s, the player after her lays down 4s, and so on. When you get all the way up to the aces, start with 2s again. The first player to lay down all her cards wins!

Note: If two girls yell "I doubt it!" at the same time, the girl to the player's left is the challenger.

Giggly Greetings

Try these funny handshakes with your friends.

Come Back Slap. Offer your palm for a friend to slap. Then turn around, slip your arm around back, and offer your palm for a second slap!

The Heart Pump. Grasp hands. Gently squeeze and relax. Squeeze and relax. Squeeze and relax.

Hand Jive. Start by slapping the palms of your right hands, **"Give me five."** Then slap the backs of your right hands, **"The other side."** Then slap left palms up high, **"Up in the air."** Then low, **"Way down there."** Big finish: Bump right hips, **"Give me some hip,"** and then left, **"Now let it slip."**

Stare Down

Sit almost nose-to-nose with a partner. Look deep into each other's eyes. No talking, laughing, or smiling. The one who keeps a straight face wins!

The Nose Knows

To play this game, you need an old sheet and at least ten friends who don't mind playing games with their noses. Hang the old sheet on a clothesline so that it touches the ground. Cut a small hole in the sheet at nose height. The hole should be just big enough for a nose to poke through. Divide your friends into two teams of at least five girls each. Have each girl poke her nose through the hole in turn, while the other team tries to guess whose nose they are seeing. The team with the most correct guesses wins!

It's a Fact: One nostril in your nose does the breathing and smelling while the other one rests.

It's a Fact: A sneeze travels at about 100 miles per hour. That's as fast as some hurricane winds!

Color a Message

Find the secret message hidden in the letters below by coloring in all the Bs, Ds, and Fs.

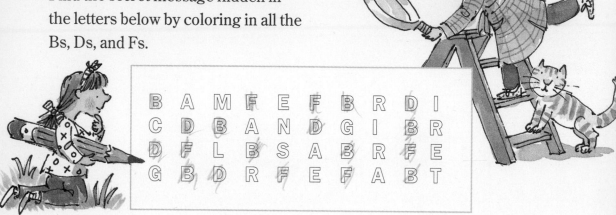

B	A	M	F	E	F	B	R	D	I
C	D	B	A	N	D	G	I	B	R
D	F	L	B	S	A	B	R	F	E
G	B	D	R	F	E	F	A	B	T

Write the secret message here:

A M E R I C A N

G I R L S A R E

G R E A T !

Color Scramble

Each of the mixed-up words below is the name of a color. Can you unscramble them?

1. erneg
2. estuuiroq
3. quaa — Aqua
4. ygra — gray
5. wloyel — yellow

6. thiwe — white
7. vyan — navy
8. groane
9. roanom
10. lotive — volite

18

Creative Coloring

Color five squares to divide this figure into five parts—one colored part and four uncolored parts. All five parts should be exactly the same size and shape.

AG Code 2

Use the American Girl decoder shown below to answer this question:

If you threw your yellow hat into the Red Sea, what would you get?

A VEr y WE T H a T !

19

Knock-knock.
Who's there?
Who.
Who who?
Did you hear an owl?

Knock-knock.
Who's there?
Scold.
Scold who?
S'cold out here.
Let me in!

Knock-knock.
Who's there?
Jamaica.
Jamaica who?
Jamaica good grade on the math test?

Knock-knock.
Who's there?
Little old lady.
Little old lady who?
I didn't know you could yodel!

Knock-knock.
Who's there?
Accordion.
Accordion who?
Accordion to the TV, it's going to rain tomorrow.

Knock-knock.
Who's there?
Ya.
Ya who?
Oh—you're glad to see me!

Tongue Twisters

Try saying these slippery sentences six times furiously fast!

A noisy noise annoys an oyster.

The sixth sheik's sixth sheep's sick.

A box of mixed biscuits, a mixed biscuit box.

She sells seashells down by the seashore.

Six small slick seals.

Ape cakes, grape cakes.

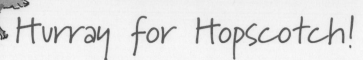

Hurray for Hopscotch!

Draw these hopscotch patterns and hop away a sunny day!

Potsy (Basic Hopscotch)

1. Use chalk to draw the Potsy pattern shown at right.

2. Toss a small stone into square 1. Then hop on all the squares except the one with the stone. With your right foot, hop into square 2 and then 3. Jump again, and land with your left foot in square 4 and your right foot in square 5. Hop the rest of the pattern in the same way.

3. Now turn around and hop back the same way. When you land in square 2, stop, bend down on one foot, pick up your stone from square 1, and hop out of the Potsy.

4. Now toss your stone into square 2 and hop through the pattern. If you miss the toss, lose your balance, or step on a line, start again.

5. Hop your way all through the numbers. When you've done square 8, you're finished!

Curly Swirly Snail

Hop through this coiled-up version of Potsy. You can rest in the "Safe Zone" in the middle. Don't get dizzy!

Chinese Hopscotch

In this game, you kick your stone instead of tossing it. Kick your stone into square 1. Then, standing on one foot, hop over square 1 and keep hopping all the way to square 10. Rest on both feet in the blank space before hopping back on the other foot to square 2. Bend down, pick up your stone, and hop out. Keep going until you've kicked your stone all the way to square 10!

Envelope Hopscotch

This game gets its name from the envelope shape at the top of the pattern.

Fruit Salad Wordsearch

The names of 20 fruits are hidden in this wordsearch. The words are forward, backward, up and down, and diagonal. After you have circled all the words, write the uncircled letters in order on the red lines below to answer this question:

Why do elephants wear red sneakers?

Word Box

apple	grapefruit	melon	pineapple
banana	kiwi	orange	plum
cherry	lemon	papaya	pomegranate
date	lime	peach	prune
grape	mango	pear	tangerine

**Note: "Apple" and "pineapple" are two separate words in this puzzle.
So are "grape" and "grapefruit."**

```
P  O  M  E  G  R  A  N  A  T  E
A  T  O  P  E  Y  R  R  E  H  C
P  H  I  L  L  D  D  A  T  E  M
A  E  P  E  P  U  P  I  N  E  M
Y  P  M  T  P  E  M  L  L  P  M
A  O  H  E  A  N  A  O  A  S  A
N  R  T  C  E  U  N  R  R  K  N
A  A  H  A  N  R  G  W  B  I  G
N  N  E  R  I  P  R  I  E  W  O
A  G  R  A  P  E  F  R  U  I  T
B  E  N  I  R  E  G  N  A  T  S
```

___ ___ ___ ___ ___ ___ ___ ___

___ ___ ___ ___ ___ ___ ___ ___!

Pizza C

In this super sneaky code, you replace each letter of the alphabet with a whole word. The words are all pizza toppings. Use this pizza

co...
at ...
co...
ow...

Twisted

Can you guess ...
these songs? ...
your favo...
song's ...

A   sauce
B   anchovies
C   mozzarella
D   tomato
E   chicken
F   green pepper
G   pork
H   onion
I   pineapple
J   sausage
K   hamburger
L   black olive
M   pepperoni
N   bacon
O   mushrooms
P   spinach
Q   broccoli
R   lettuce
S   green olive
T   pesto
U   shrimp
V   goat cheese
W   sardines
X   oregano
Y   pine nuts
Z   eggplant

I ' M   H   U   N   G   R   Y !

pineapple pepperoni onion shrimp bacon pork lettuce pine nuts

Tunes

...the real names of
... Then try singing
...rite using the
...s twisted title!

1. **Drizzle, Drizzle, Disappear**
   Answer: Rain, Rain, Go Away

2. **Sparkle, Sparkle,
   Tiny Five-Pointed Figure**
   Answer:

3. **Paddle, Paddle, Paddle the Ship
   Belonging to You**
   Answer:

4. **Five Plus One Tiny Quackers**
   Answer:

5. **Bring My Being to the Playing Diamond**
   Answer:

6. **Joyous Date of Arrival into the World**
   Answer:

7. **This Ancient Male**
   Answer:

8. **Bleat, Bleat, Dark Woolly Creature**
   Answer:

Name Game

Make up your own bouncy verse for each letter of the alphabet. Bounce a ball under one of your legs as you say each name. Here are a few verses to get you started:

A My name is Anna.
My husband's name is Al.
We live in Alabama.
And we sell apples.

B My name is Becky.
My husband's name is Bill.
We live in Burlington.
And we sell basketballs.

C My name is Cara.
My husband's name is Carl.
We live in California.
And we sell cantaloupes.

Music Match

Play this game with at least seven friends. Before you play, think of songs that everyone knows. Write down each song title on two separate slips of paper. Pass out the slips of paper, but don't let your friends see one another's titles. Then tell each friend to walk around humming her song and listening for the other girl who is humming it. The pair of girls who find each other first are the winners.

Hats, Hats, Hats!

Use what's under your hat to solve this puzzle! If you need a hint, look in the word box!

Across

1. A baby's hat.
2. A genie's hat.
3. A Monopoly® playing piece.
4. A Mexican hat.
5. A biker's hat.
6. A funny little hat.

Down

4. A cowboy's hat.
7. A hat that's attached to a jacket.
8. A square of cloth.
9. A hat for the game.
10. A hat made from grass.

Word Box

baseball cap	beanie	bonnet	helmet
hood	sombrero	stetson	straw hat
top hat	turban	kerchief	

Art Lesson

Sharpen your colored pencils and get ready to draw:

1. a portly pig

2. a playful puppy

3. a rollerskating turtle

4. a curious cat

Mystery Sentence

Insert the same letter in the seven blanks below to solve this mystery sentence.

_A_ _I_ _RAW _IZZY _INOSAURS.

Sign Time

Mary Catherine O'Neal was tired of signing her name the same old way. So she wrote down her initials and turned them into the picture below! Now her friends call her Mary Cat for short. Can you find a way to turn your initials into a picture?

Dots and Squares

For this game, you need paper, a pencil, and one or more friends. You play on a grid of dots. Each player, in turn, draws a line connecting two dots. No diagonal lines! When you draw a line that completes a square, write your initial inside and draw another line. The player with the most squares at the end wins. Play a practice game on the little grid above to get the idea.

Autograph Album

Kylie got a new autograph album and all her friends signed it. Can you read the messages on the turquoise pages? Add your own messages on the yellow pages.

YYUR
YYUB
I CUR
YY4ME
Becky

URAQT INVU
2 GOOD 2B
4 GOTTEN
Catalin

Read   see
up   will
and   you
down   and
Danita

that
I
like
you

me
like
you
if

It makes me giggle.
It makes me laugh
To think you want my autograph.
Yours till Niagara Falls,
Jasmine

I love you little.
I love you big.
I love you like a little pig.
Yours till the cows come home,
Emily

There are gold ships,
There are silver ships,
But there's no ship
like friendship.
Tania

You be the ice cream, I'll be the
freezer.
You be the lemon, I'll be the
squeezer.
Kenesha

Some write for pleasure,
Some write for fame,
But I write only
To sign my name.
♡ Andrea

Remember the girl in the city,
Remember the girl in the town,
Remember the girl who spoiled
your book
By writing it up-side-down.
Meredith

Study hard, don't be a flop!
Sooner or later you'll
reach the top!
Maya

Can't think.
Brain numb.
Inspiration won't come.
Poor ink, bad pen.
That's all. Amen!
Lauren

Backwords

Use the clues to figure out what word fills the blanks on the first line of each puzzle. When you spell that word backward, it will complete the phrase on the second line of each puzzle. The first one is done for you.

1. opposite of go: __S__ __T__ __O__ __P__

   backword: pans and __P__ __O__ __T__ __S__

2. someone who doesn't tell the truth: ___ ___ ___ ___

   backword: a train runs on a ___ ___ ___ ___

3. a sticky black substance: ___ ___ ___

   backword: a kind of rodent ___ ___ ___

4. a puppy bite: ___ ___ ___

   backword: a safety ___ ___ ___

Grizzly Bear

Maria and Johanna are playing a game. Can you figure out the pattern?

Maria: **Grizzly bear.**
Johanna: **Hairdresser.**
Maria: **Earthquake.**
Johanna: **Aching head.**
Maria: **Editor.**
Johanna: **Urgent telegram.**
Maria: **America the Beautiful!**

Extraordinary!

Extraordinary means "remarkable, unusual, outstanding." How many words can you make using the letters in the word **EXTRAORDINARY**? If you can find more than 50 words, you're extraordinary!

Two-Letter Test

Try this test with a friend. You'll need a timer, plus some paper and pencils for both of you. Set the timer for two minutes. Then see who can come up with more two-letter words before time runs out.

Word Wheel

There are 18 words of three or more letters hidden around the word wheel. How many can you find? The letters have to be together and in the right order. Start with the word *reach*.

Tic-Tac-Addition

In this version of tic-tac-toe, you use numbers instead of Xs and Os. The object is to be the first player to complete a row in any direction that adds up to a certain number.

Decide what the number will be before you begin. It can be any number from 13 to 20. One player can play with only these even numbers: 2, 4, 6, 8, 10. The other player uses only these odd numbers: 1, 3, 5, 7, 9. A number can be used only once. Each player, in turn, writes a number in any space on the tic-tac-toe grid. The winner shouts, "Tic-tac-addition!"

★

Brainbenders

1. It's early in the morning and you are getting dressed in the dark. In your sock drawer are ten purple socks and ten yellow socks. How many socks must you take out of the drawer to be sure you have a pair of yellow socks?

2. A lollipop and a box of candy cost $1.10. The box of candy costs exactly one dollar more than the lollipop. What did the box of candy cost?

3. How can you take eight 8s and make them add up to 1,000?

Buzz!

The faster you and your friends play this game, the more you'll sound like a busy, buzzing beehive! Players take turns counting, but say "buzz" instead of any number that has 7 in it or is a multiple of 7 (7, 14, 17, 21, 27, and so on). A player who misses a "buzz" is out. Don't get stung!

Example:

1, 2, 3, 4, 5, 6, *BUZZ!*, 8, 9, 10, 11, 12, 13, *BUZZ!*, 15, 16, *BUZZ!* ...

Fizz-Buzz!

If you like Buzz, try this more challenging version. Players say "buzz" for numbers with 7 and multiples of 7 and "fizz" for numbers with 5 and multiples of 5.

Example:

1, 2, 3, 4, *FIZZ!*, 6, *BUZZ!*, 8, 9, *FIZZ!*, 11, 12, 13, *BUZZ!*, *FIZZ!* ...

Knot So!

This trick is simple, once you know the secret. Lay a piece of string that's about 3 feet long on a table. Dare your friends to tie the string into a knot *without letting go of either end.* Here's how to do it:

Clip Trick

Scientists haven't been able to explain why this trick works, but it works every time!

1. Fold a dollar bill and clip two paper clips to it, exactly as shown.

2. Pull the two ends of the dollar quickly. The paper clips will pop off into the air—joined together!

1. Fold your arms across your chest, with your left hand on top of your right arm, and your right hand tucked under your left arm.

2. With your arms still crossed, pick up the string—one end in your right hand, one end in your left.

3. Uncross your arms and bring your hands out in front of you. Congratulations! You've tied the knot!

C.A.R.

Get ready to be amazing. You'll be able to show your friends three objects, leave the room while they pick one, and then return to tell them which object they picked. And you'll be right every time. To do this, you have to be a bit sneaky, which is the secret to all great magic tricks. Here's what you do:

In private.

Practice with a partner. The key to this trick is the word "C.A.R." After you've left the room and the audience has picked an object, your partner calls you back with one of three phrases. If she says, "**C**ome in," the audience picked the first object. If she says, "**A**ll right," they picked the second. If she says, "**R**eady," they picked the third. Practice until your routine is flawless.

In front of an audience.

With magic tricks, presentation is everything. Do the trick just as you practiced, but with plenty of pizzazz. Slowly wave your hands over the objects. Hold your hand to your forehead as you concentrate. Let the suspense build. Announce your answer, and then bask in the applause.

Grandma's Attic Wordsearch

Sneak a peek in Grandma's attic and see what you can find. The items you see there are hidden in the wordsearch on the next page. You'll find words forward, backward, and up and down. When you find the name of an item in the wordsearch, circle it. The words you are looking for are in the word box below. Can you find them all?

Word Box

cane	hats	trunk	camera	spinning wheel
telephone	desk	sword	radio	snowshoes
books	chair	rake	newspapers	golf bag
teddy bear	boxes	roller skates	hip boots	rocking horse
robes	rag			

Word search puzzle grid:

```
W R O B E S   W O R D   N A E
A U X O M A I R A K E I O N E
W R E C I S P R H K D T N E W S
R O H K S N B A O H S O E A P
T L A O C I G R X E N S R W A
E L I B A N G R O E N N A A P
D E R O C G O X F R N A G E E
D R G E L N B E U N B E G R R
Y S K L A H R A A D K N T S S
B K T A N E D A D P N A E H
E A C N M E W R K H A W E D
A T A D E L H D A E N G S A
R E N E L O E P H N E E H D
P S T O O B P I H S A
```

Scavenger Hunt

You and your friends can have a great scavenger hunt—rain or shine! Get together with at least three friends and divide into two teams. Cut out the lists on the next page and give one list to each team. Use the rainy day list for an indoor hunt, or turn the list over to the sunny side for an outdoor hunt. The team that finds the most items in 15 minutes wins!

Rainy Day Hunt

- [x] 1. something purple
- [x] 2. a hat
- [x] 3. something musical
- [ ] 4. dice
- [ ] 5. something gold
- [x] 6. a stuffed animal
- [ ] 7. thread that is not black or white
- [ ] 8. a postcard
- [x] 9. a marker or pen
- [ ] 10. lace
- [ ] 11. something more than 30 years old
- [ ] 12. something with a price tag still on it
- [ ] 13. something with 4 wheels
- [ ] 14. a picture of an animal
- [ ] 15. a picture of a baby
- [ ] 16. something made of rubber
- [ ] 17. a pair of sunglasses
- [ ] 18. something with a heart on it
- [x] 19. something that bounces
- [ ] 20. a book with more than 300 pages

Rainy Day Hunt

- [ ] 1. something purple
- [ ] 2. a hat
- [ ] 3. something musical
- [ ] 4. dice
- [ ] 5. something gold
- [ ] 6. a stuffed animal
- [ ] 7. thread that is not black or white
- [ ] 8. a postcard
- [ ] 9. a marker or pen
- [ ] 10. lace
- [ ] 11. something more than 30 years old
- [ ] 12. something with a price tag still on it
- [ ] 13. something with 4 wheels
- [ ] 14. a picture of an animal
- [ ] 15. a picture of a baby
- [ ] 16. something made of rubber
- [ ] 17. a pair of sunglasses
- [ ] 18. something with a heart on it
- [ ] 19. something that bounces
- [ ] 20. a book with more than 300 pages

Sunny Day Hunt

☐ **1.** a stone
☐ **2.** a leaf
☐ **3.** something that rolls
☐ **4.** a twig
☐ **5.** a white flower
☐ **6.** a yellow flower
☐ **7.** a seed
☐ **8.** something black and white
☐ **9.** a mud pie
☐ **10.** a blade of grass
☐ **11.** something smooth
☐ **12.** sand
☐ **13.** a bottle cap
☐ **14.** an aluminum can
☐ **15.** a bug
☐ **16.** something that begins
  with "S"
☐ **17.** something made of wood
☐ **18.** a feather
☐ **19.** something shiny
☐ **20.** something that makes noise

Sunny Day Hunt

☐ **1.** a stone
☐ **2.** a leaf
☐ **3.** something that rolls
☐ **4.** a twig
☐ **5.** a white flower
☐ **6.** a yellow flower
☐ **7.** a seed
☐ **8.** something black and white
☐ **9.** a mud pie
☐ **10.** a blade of grass
☐ **11.** something smooth
☐ **12.** sand
☐ **13.** a bottle cap
☐ **14.** an aluminum can
☐ **15.** a bug
☐ **16.** something that begins
  with "S"
☐ **17.** something made of wood
☐ **18.** a feather
☐ **19.** something shiny
☐ **20.** something that makes noise

Line Designs

Trace these designs completely, without lifting your pen or pencil and without tracing over any part twice.

1.

2.

3.

4.

5.

Famous Girls Crossword

The answers to these crossword clues are the names of famous girls from books and movies!

Word Box

Ramona	Anna	Heidi	Minnie
Alice	Laura	Dorothy	Annie
Tinkerbelle	Fern	Matilda	Mary
Wendy			

Across

1. All she had to do to get home was click her ruby slippers together.
4. She starts off school as a pest in kindergarten.
6. She finds more than flowers in a secret place on a big estate.
7. She comes to love her gruff grandfather in the Swiss Alps.
10. The Queen of Hearts gives her a headache.
11. Charlotte the spider and Wilbur the pig are her friends.
12. Her father finds a wife from Maine who is plain and tall.

Down

2. You clap to save her life.
3. A little house on the prairie is _____ Ingalls's home.
5. She sings, "The sun'll come out tomorrow."
6. She is a famous cartoon mouse.
8. The Trunchbull is her mean headmistress.
9. _____ Darling sews on Peter's shadow and then flies home with him.

We're There!

Bored in the backseat on a long car trip? This is the game for you. Pick out an object or landmark up ahead. Then close your eyes. When you think you've reached the thing you spotted, say "We're there!" and open your eyes. How close were you?

NEXT REST AREA
267 miles

25

Still bored? Try this car game with your family. Take turns spotting the numbers 1 through 25 on the license plates of passing cars. Start by checking for the number 1 on the license plate of the first car that passes. If there's a 1 on the plate, you get to check the next car for a 2. If you don't see a 1 on the plate, it's the next player's turn. The first player to reach 25 wins!

City Scramble

Lots of people have nicknames, but did you know that
some cities have nicknames, too? Look at the nicknames below, at left.
Then unscramble the letters at right to find out the real names of the cities.

1. **The Big Apple**......................EWN KORY
2. **Beantown**................................TSBOON
3. **The Motor City**.................OERTDIT
4. **The Big Easy**........................WNE LNERASO
5. **The Windy City**..................GCCIOAH

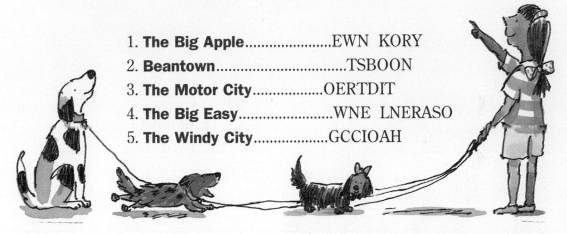

---- ★ ----

Mystery Plates

See if you can guess who these cars
belong to. For example, the car with the
license plate NPOLE belongs to Santa.
Make up some of your own, too!

HUFNPUF

NPOLE

SHEEP COMEHOME

JANE&ME

APPLESYES

Tag with a Twist

Try these new twists on an old favorite!

Flashlight Tag

Play this game when it's dark. You tag another player by shining a flashlight on her and calling out her name.

Air Tag

You can tag another player only if part of the player is touching the ground.

Shadow Tag

Tag another player by stepping on her shadow.

Hospital Tag

When you tag another player, she must keep her hand on her body where you tagged her. She becomes IT and must keep her hand there until she tags another player.

Chain Tag

When you tag another player, she links arms with you as you chase after the other girls. As you tag more players, the chain gets longer and longer. When the last player is tagged, the game starts again. The first player you tagged becomes IT.

Bubble Blowout

Ordinary things around your house make great bubble blowers!

- Thin copper wire bent into wands of different shapes
- A kitchen funnel
- A drinking straw
- A cardboard tube
- The bottom of a plastic berry container (makes lots of tiny bubbles)

Bubble Up!

It's easy to whip up your own bubble potion. You'll need:

- Clean plastic gallon jug
- Funnel
- Measuring cup with spout
- 6 cups water
- 2 cups Joy® liquid dish soap
- ¾ cup of white Karo® syrup

1. Uncap the plastic jug. Place the funnel in the mouth of the jug.

2. Have an adult help you measure and pour the water, dish soap, and syrup into the jug.

3. Put the cap on the jug, and shake it to mix the ingredients.

4. Pour some of the bubble potion into a small dish, and you're ready to blow!

It's a fact: The biggest soap bubble on record was 50 feet long!

Bubblemania

Can you fill in the blanks in the poem? The same letters are used to make the missing word for each blank.

Jill was blowing bubbles
and she said she'd never _____.
She loved to watch them swell up
and she loved to watch them pop.
She had two big _____ of bubble juice
and that was quite a lot.
"Until this goop is gone," she said,
"I won't budge from this _____."

Bubble Trouble

Consuela's bath has overflowed with bubbles! Rub-a-dub-dub, help her get to the tub!

Cross-Outs

Cross out the words in the boxes below that answer each question at right. The words that are left will answer this riddle:

A softball player is on third base. What's her favorite saying?

1. Cross out 3 sports.
2. Cross out 3 weather words.
3. Cross out 4 colors.
4. Cross out 2 things that fly.
5. Cross out 3 words that rhyme with eight.

soccer	scarlet	straight	cloudy	rain
weight	baseball	no	turquoise	like
jet	grate	aqua	purple	tennis
sunny	there's	place	bluebird	home

Field Day Fun

Jill, Sydney, Barb, and Yasmin have won the four top prizes in the 50-yard dash. Read the clues to figure out which girl came in first, second, third, and fourth.

- A tall girl came in fourth place.
- A girl with straight hair came in second.
- A girl wearing shorts came in first.
- Sydney came in just after Barb.

Jill   Sydney   Barb   Yasmin

First: _____ Second: _____ Third: _____ Fourth: _____

Letter Finish

Add straight lines to the unfinished letters at right to make the names of six sports.

Ready? Set? Go!

GO_F
30∧_∣∖G
⊤E∖∖S
_OC<E∨
G∨∨∣-S⊤ICS
FOO⊤3_-__

AG Code 3

Montana came home for supper after her softball team won the championship game. She put ketchup and relish on one hot dog and mustard on another.

"Congratulations, Champ!" said her father. How did he know her team had won? Use the decoder to find out the answer.

⊓⊓ ∨⊐⊔⊐ ⊐⊔ ⊐⊓⊓ ⊐⊔∧⊓!
H E ___ ___ ___ ___ ___ ___ ___ ___ ___!

Tricky Type

Can you guess the words, phrases, or sayings from the way the letters are arranged in the boxes below? For example, the answer to number 1 is "Grown up."

1. NWORG

2. FRIEND fight FRIEND

3. ROSIE

4. Dough

5. RETTAB

6. ever
ever
ever
ever

7. CHANCE

8. D
N at 'em
A

9. hang

| 10. | 11. | 12. |
| M Y R R E | MOVIE | LAST |

| 13. | 14. | 15. |
| BUCKLE ↑ | WORDS WORDS | thing thing |

| 16. | 17. | 18. |
| FIVE | temp e rature | TIRE |

Fairy Tale Wordsearch

Search the castle on the right to find all 16 words hidden in this wordsearch. The words are forward, backward, upside down, and diagonal. Check the word box if you need hints.

Word Box

ball	elf	magic	spell
castle	fairy	prince	wand
coach	gnome	princess	witch
crown	king	queen	wizard

 Twisted Tales

Can you guess the real names of these twisted tales?

1. **Two Plus One Tiny Oinkers**
   Answer: The Three Little Pigs

2. **Ancient Female Who Resided in Footwear**
   Answer:

3. **Snoozing Pretty One**
   Answer:

4. **The Slow-Moving, Hard-Shelled Creature and the Cottontail**
   Answer:

5. **The Unattractive Young Quacker**
   Answer:

6. **The Imperial Ruler's Just-Purchased Garments**
   Answer:

7. **The Feline in the Cap**
   Answer:

8. **The Daughter of the King and the Small Round Green Vegetable**
   Answer:

P E L F A W I T C H
R R H A A N C D O B
I S I O M I E P A R
N K I N G Z R L C N
C C E A C C L Y H Q
E C M S P E L L A U
M R E A C A S T L E
N O D K Y S Z S E E
D W I Z A R D H E N
G N O M E D N A W R

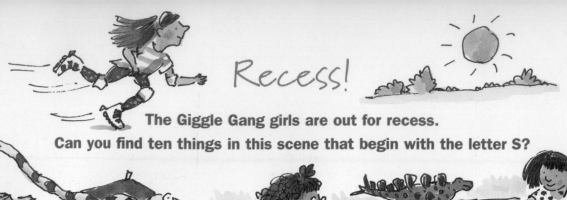

Recess!

The Giggle Gang girls are out for recess.
Can you find ten things in this scene that begin with the letter S?

Statues

You don't need any equipment for this playground favorite. Get together with three or four friends and choose one person to be the "sculptor." The sculptor twirls each player around a few times and then lets go. Then that player freezes into a statue. Each player must hold her pose until everyone has been twirled. Then the sculptor picks her favorite statue to become the next sculptor. The sillier the poses, the better!

Mushpot

You can play this game with your whole class—all you need is a rubber playground ball. Everyone makes a big circle, and five players volunteer to go into the *mushpot,* or middle of the circle. The players on the outside of the circle throw the ball to try to hit the players in the mushpot. If a player in the mushpot gets hit, she joins the players on the outside of the circle. The last player left in the mushpot wins!

After-School Crossword

The answers to these crossword clues are things American girls do or play with after school.

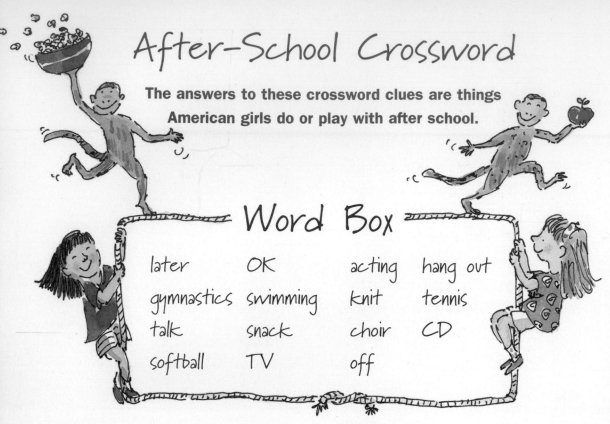

Word Box

later	OK	acting	hang out
gymnastics	swimming	knit	tennis
talk	snack	choir	CD
softball	TV	off	

Across

1. If you don't have anything else to do, just _____ _____ at home.
4. You'll turn into a sofa spud if you spend too much time in front of this.
5. You do the butterfly and the crawl in this sport.
7. These lessons can help you on stage.
8. Ask your grandma to teach you to _____ socks.
9. Join one if you like to sing.
12. It involves a diamond, but it's not a card game.

Down

2. In this sport, you jump over a horse that doesn't move.
3. You can play singles or doubles.
4. _____ on the phone.
5. Yum, yum! Try to have a healthy one.
6. What you tell Mom when she asks, "When will you do your homework?"
9. Listen to your favorite songs on a _____ player.
10. What you hope Mom says when a friend asks you over.
11. Goof _____.

To the Pet Shop!

Molly's parents said she could have a puppy! Help her get to the pet shop to pick out her pup.

What name has Molly picked out for her puppy? To find out, look at the stores in the order she passed them. If she went by the door, write down the first letter of the store.

S C O U T

Scrambled Doggies

Unscramble the letters to write the names of eight kinds of dogs. Check the word box below if you need help.

1. mlaadtina

_____

2. gleabe

_____

3. xbore

_____

4. loopde

_____

5. ylısku

_____

6. rrreite

_____

7. pansiel

_____

8. rrreteive

_____

Word Box

terrier   poodle
spaniel   beagle
husky   boxer
retriever dalmatian

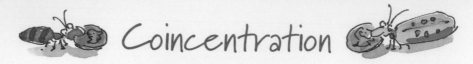

Coincentration

Which circle is the same size as a penny? A dime? A nickel? A quarter?
Use real coins to check your answers.

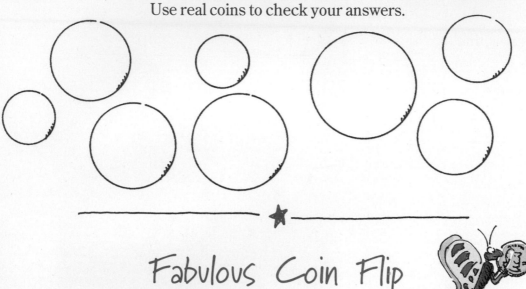

---★---

Fabulous Coin Flip

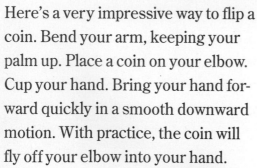

Here's a very impressive way to flip a coin. Bend your arm, keeping your palm up. Place a coin on your elbow. Cup your hand. Bring your hand forward quickly in a smooth downward motion. With practice, the coin will fly off your elbow into your hand.

Crazy Coin Trick

Place six coins in a row, like this:

Turn over two coins at a time. In just three moves, try to rearrange the coins so they look like this:

Dimes to Pennies

Put a dime on spot 1 and on spot 3. Put a penny on spot 6 and on spot 8. One at a time, move the coins along the lines from one spot to another.

Try to get the dimes on spots 6 and 8 and the pennies on spots 1 and 3. Only one coin at a time may be on a spot.

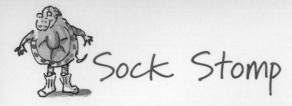

Sock Stomp

Get ready for some foot-stomping, sock-flopping fun! You can play this game with as few as two people, but it's more fun with a crowd. To play, all players take off their shoes and pull their socks out a few inches so the toes are floppy. When you say "go," the stomping begins. Watch out for toes! The last player left with a sock on is the winner.

Finger Calculator

This trick magically turns your hands into a calculator that can multiply by nine. Here's how: First, draw calculator buttons on your hands, like those shown below.

Then tell a friend she can multiply a single-digit number by nine by pressing the buttons on your hands. For example, try nine times three. Have your friend press ON, then the buttons for 9, x, and 3. After she presses the = button, lower the finger that was multiplied by nine.

The fingers left standing tell the answer! There are 2 fingers standing to the left of the finger that's down, and 7 fingers standing to the right. 9 x 3 = 27!

Shoe Detective

You can tell a lot about a girl from the shoes she wears. For this game, choose someone to be the shoe detective and ask her to leave the room. While she's gone, the rest of the players put their shoes in a pile in the middle of the floor. Then call the shoe detective back. She chooses a shoe from the pile, and then tells one or two things she has figured out about the person who wears that

shoe. For example, if it's a tennis shoe, the person probably likes sports. If the sole is worn down, the owner might walk a lot. Use your imagination!

AG Code 4

Use the decoder on the right to answer this question:
Why isn't your hand 12 inches long?

B E _ _ _ _ _ _ _

_ _ _ _ _ _ _ _ _ _ _ _ _

_ _ _ _ _ _ _ _ _

_ _ _ _ _ _ _ _ !

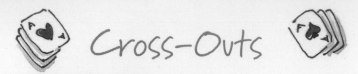

Cross-Outs

What do you put on a table and cut, but not eat? The answer's hidden in the box below. Follow the instructions on the right. Then read what's left, and the answer's in sight!

1. Cross out 3 animals.
2. Cross out 5 adjectives.
3. Cross out 2 girls' names.
4. Cross out 2 words that contain the letters "I," "P," and "L."
5. Cross out 4 jobs that people do.

cat	lip	gardener	of	fabulous
a	lawyer	pill	angry	author
teacher	busy	pony	lively	raccoon
prickly	deck	Amy	cards	Erin

Twin Test

Study the rows of playing cards at right. In each row, there are two cards that are exactly alike. Can you find them?

Step into a Playing Card

This trick is very simple, very showy, and very, very good. The best part is that no one will believe it's possible—until you show them. All you need are a pair of scissors and some old playing cards. Practice in private first. Here's what to do:

1. Fold a card lengthwise.

2. Make a series of cuts as shown.

3. Cut along the fold from A to B.

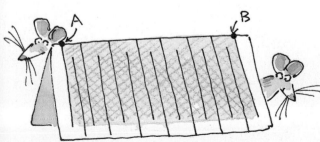

4. Open the card. You've made a large ring. Step into it and take a bow!

71

Quick Dip Maze

It's hot, hot, hot! Draw a line
to get Bess to the beach.

SNACK BAR

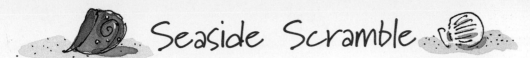

Seaside Scramble

Use the clues to help you unscramble these things you might find in or near the sea.

1. A bird that lives near the sea. ULLGASE

2. A creature with claws that crawls sideways along the sand. BRAC

3. A long fish that looks like a snake. ELE

4. A big-eyed creature with eight arms. OSTUPCO

5. A plant that grows underwater. AESWEDE

6. It's not a fish, but it lives in the sea. WEHLA

7. If you break off one of this creature's five arms, it will grow back. SIAHRSTF

8. Watch out for this dangerous fish! AKSHR

Swims

There's something special about this word:

SWIMS

Can you guess what it is? Turn the page upside down to find out the answer.

It looks the same upside down or right side up.

It's a Fact: The tallest sand castle ever built was 56 feet, 2 inches tall. It was built in 1989 by 2,000 people in Kaseda, Japan!

Ghost

This word game is for 2 to 4 players.
The object is to add letters together to make someone else spell a word,
without spelling one yourself. Here's how it goes:

1. The first player thinks of a word. Let's say she picks *water.* Then she says the first letter of that word out loud.

2. The second player thinks of a word that starts with W. Let's say she picks *woman.* Then she says the first two letters of her word out loud.

3. Player three thinks of the word *worm*, and says the first three letters of her word out loud.

4. This is where the game gets tricky. Player four could do one of three things:

Force another player to spell a word. If player four adds the letter L, she forces player five to spell *world* and lose the round.

Bluff. If player four can't think of a word, she could add any letter to try to fool the other players. But if another player challenges her, she must name the word that starts with those letters. If she can't, she loses the round.

As a last resort, spell a word. If player four adds an M, she'll spell the word *worm* and lose the round. If a player loses a round, she gets a G. After her second loss she gets an H, and so on until she collects all the letters that spell GHOST. Use paper and pencil to keep track of everyone's "ghost" letters. The last player to become a "ghost" wins!

Sweet Tooth Crossword

Word Box

hermits	licorice	kitchen	iced	Ruth	sherbet
pear	set	crust	graham	ah	rhubarb
pain	jube	peanuts	mint	marsh	sugar
end	coconut	lion	bean	gum	syrup
rock candy				chocolate cake	

Across

1. A common birthday treat
7. _____ _____ mountain
8. Another word for frosted
9. You might find one among your animal crackers.
10. Baby _____ candy bar
11. A jelly _____
12. If pudding doesn't do this, it will be runny.
13. Part of a pie
15. Maple _____
17. Kind of cracker
19. Sound you make when your sweet tooth is satisfied
20. You chew it but don't swallow it.
24. Kind of pie
25. Another name for goobers

Down

2. Bar cookies with nuts and raisins
3. Comes from a palm tree
4. Red or black _____
5. The part of a candy bar you hate to come to
6. Lots of desserts are made here.
14. Dessert similar to ice cream
15. This ingredient is in most sweets.
16. Fruit sometimes used in tarts
18. _____ mallow
21. An after-dinner _____
22. Ju_____
23. What your tummy gets if you overdo the sweets

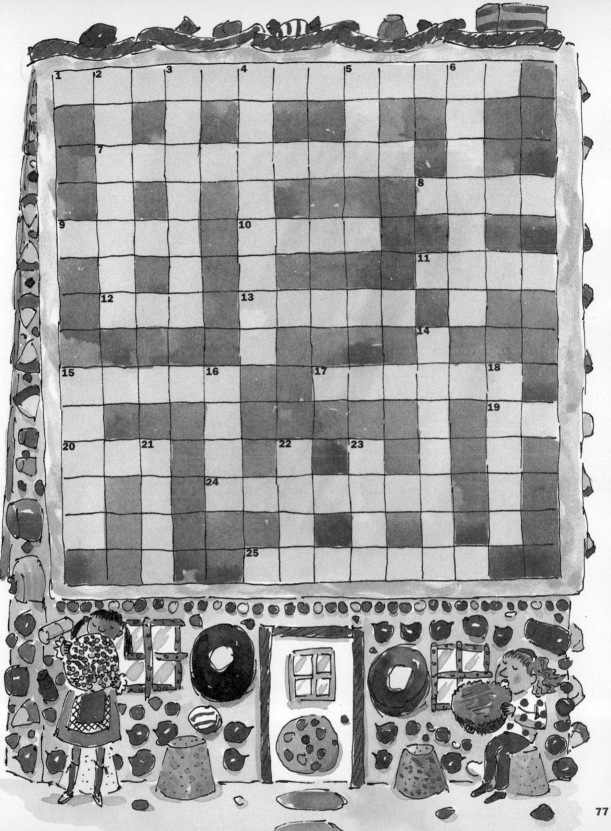

Toothpick Tricks

Try to solve these tricky toothpick puzzles!
You might want to arrange real toothpicks in these patterns.
Then you can move them around as you figure out the answer.

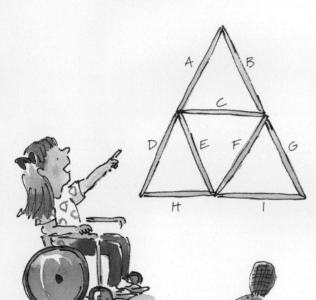

1. Take away three toothpicks to leave two triangles.
2. Take away three toothpicks to leave only one triangle.

3. Take away four toothpicks to leave two equal squares.
4. Take away four toothpicks to leave only one square.

5. Take away four toothpicks to leave four triangles all the same size.

6. Move only three toothpicks to make the fish swim in the opposite direction.

Brainbenders

1. Which month has 28 days?

2. When did Christmas Day and New Year's Day fall in the same year?

3. Where does Thursday come before Wednesday?

4. Which is correct: 16 + 9 *is* 24 or 16 + 9 *are* 24?

5. Why are 1993 pennies worth almost 20 dollars?

6. Which is heavier—a pound of feathers or a pound of rocks?

7. Jennifer thinks she's awesome at spelling, but she can't find the word that's mispelled on this page. Can you?

8. Lindsey has two coins in her pocket that add up to 30 cents. One coin is not a nickel. What are the two coins?

Clean Up!

The Giggle Gang girls are having a slumber party and making a big mess!
Look at the picture carefully. Then turn the page to test your memory!

Clean Up!

Make a list of five things the Giggle Gang girls need to clean up. When you finish your list, turn back to page 81 to check your answers.

Smooth Moves

The sillier this game gets, the better. Have all your guests stand in a circle. Start by making any movement, such as putting your fingers in your ears. The girl to your right has to copy your move exactly. Then she adds one of her own, like hopping up and down on one foot. The next girl copies both those moves and adds another. If a player forgets a move, she sits down. The last player left standing wins!

Sleeping Bag Shimmy

Here's one more sure-fire slumber-party pleaser. Set up an obstacle course for your guests to shimmy through in their sleeping bags!

Include tables to wiggle under and chairs to scooch around. Soon everyone will be wriggling and giggling across the floor!

Answers

Page 2
Game Time!

1. Eleven
2. Long hair
3. Checkers
4. Purple
5. Brown and white, a ball
6. Three
7. Five

Wacky Wordsearch

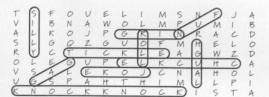

Pages 4, 5
Games Galore Crossword

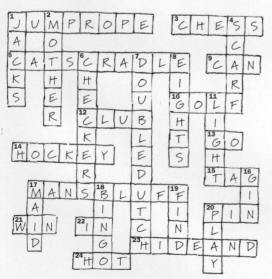

Page 7
Appearances Can Be Deceiving

a, appear, pea, ear, pear, ran, an

Eye Foolers

1. Both squares are the same size.
2. Both lines are the same length.
3. Both circles are the same size.

Page 8
To the Airport!

Page 9
AG Code 1

Alaska my mother!

Pages 10, 11
Tricky Type

1. Three little pigs
2. Broken heart
3. Stuck up
4. Peanut butter and jelly sandwich
5. Double trouble
6. Three strikes and you're out
7. Shame on you
8. Holy cow
9. Falling in love
10. Sloppy Joe's
11. Spring fever
12. Me and my shadow
13. Rule of thumb
14. History repeats itself
15. Comic strips
16. Bagpipes
17. Amazing grace
18. Coconut

Page 12
Magic 15

Possible answer:

8	1	6
3	5	7
4	9	2

Page 13
Triangle Tangle

15

Hidden Numbers

1. At camp we have fu**n in** e**v**ery kind of weather. [9]
2. Pa**t won** the road race. [2]
3. Becca swim**s even** when the sun isn't shining. [7]
4. I made our neighbor's dog get o**ff our** porch. [4]
5. Brittany's h**eight** helps her get basket after basket. [8]
6. Bo**th ree**ls for my fishing rod are broken. [3]
7. There was a goldfinch **on e**ach perch of the feeder. [1]

Page 18
Color a Message

American girls are great!

Color Scramble

1. green
2. turquoise
3. aqua
4. gray
5. yellow
6. white
7. navy
8. orange
9. maroon
10. violet

Page 19
Creative Coloring

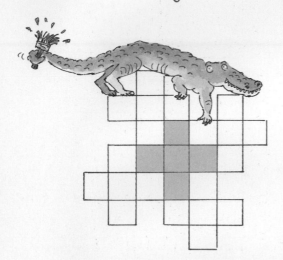

AG Code 2

A very wet hat!

Page 24
Fruit Salad Wordsearch

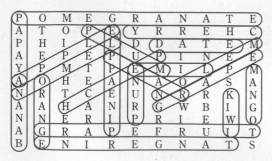

To hide in the strawberries!

Page 25
Pizza Code

I'm hungry!

Page 26
Twisted Tunes

1. Rain, Rain, Go Away
2. Twinkle, Twinkle, Little Star
3. Row, Row, Row Your Boat
4. Six Little Ducks
5. Take Me Out to the Ballgame
6. Happy Birthday
7. This Old Man
8. Baa, Baa, Black Sheep

Pages 28, 29
Hats, Hats, Hats!

Page 31
Mystery Sentence

The missing letter is D.

Dad did draw dizzy dinosaurs.

Page 32

Autograph Album

Too wise you are,
Too wise you be,
I see you are
Too wise for me.
Becky

You are a cutie. I envy you.
Too good to be forgotten.
Catalin

Read up and down and you will see
That I like you if you like me.
Danita

Page 34

Backwords

1. stop, pots
2. liar, rail
3. tar, rat
4. nip, pin

Grizzly Bear

Each girl takes the ending sound from the last word or phrase and uses it as the beginning sound of her own word or phrase.

Page 35

Extraordinary!

Possible answers:

a, air, airy, an, ant, are, art, at, ate, ax, dainty, dairy, darn, dart, date, day, dine, do, drain, drat, ear, earn, eat, edit, editor, exit, extra, I, idea, in, into, it, nay, near, neat, net, next, no, nod, not, note, oar, oat, ordinary, ox, oxen, raid, rain, ran, rat, rate, ray, rent, rid, ride, riot, road, roar, rod, rot, tad, tan, tar, tax, tear, tide, tie, tin, to, toe, tone, tore, torn, toy, trade, train, tray, trio, yarn, year, yearn, yen, yet

Two-Letter Test

Possible answers:

ad, ah, am, an, as, at, ax, be, by, do, go, ha, hi, if, in, is, it, la, me, my, no, oh, on, or, ox, Oz, so, to, up, us, we

Word Wheel

reach, reaches, each, ache, aches, chest, strain, strains, train, trains, rain, rains, see, seep, plate, late, later, ate

Page 36

Brainbenders

1. Twelve—the first ten socks could all be purple.
2. The box of candy costs $1.05.
3. $$\begin{array}{r} 8 \\ 8 \\ 8 \\ 88 \\ +888 \\ \hline 1{,}000 \end{array}$$

Pages 40, 41

Grandma's Attic Wordsearch

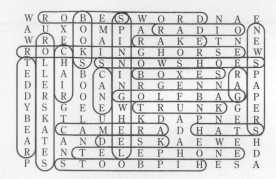

Page 45

Line Designs

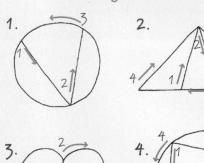

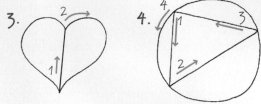

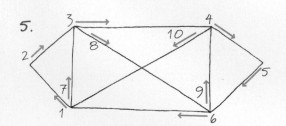

Pages 46, 47

Famous Girls Crossword

Across

1. **Dorothy** from *The Wizard of Oz* by L. Frank Baum

4. **Ramona** from stories by Beverly Cleary

6. **Mary** from *The Secret Garden* by Frances Hodgson Burnett

7. *Heidi* by Johanna Spyri

10. **Alice** from *Alice in Wonderland* by Lewis Carroll

11. **Fern** from *Charlotte's Web* by E. B. White

12. **Anna** from *Sarah, Plain and Tall* by Patricia MacLachlan

Down

2. **Tinkerbelle** from *Peter Pan* by J. M. Barrie

3. **Laura** from *Little House on the Prairie* by Laura Ingalls Wilder

5. **Annie** from the musical *Annie*

6. **Minnie** Mouse

8. *Matilda* by Roald Dahl

9. **Wendy** from *Peter Pan* by J. M. Barrie

Page 49

City Scramble

1. New York
2. Boston
3. Detroit
4. New Orleans
5. Chicago

Mystery Plates

1. **HUFNPUF:** Big Bad Wolf
2. **NPOLE:** Santa
3. **SHEEPCOMEHOME:** Bo Peep
4. **JANE&ME:** Tarzan
5. **APPLESYES:** Johnny Appleseed

Page 53
Bubblemania

Stop, pots, spot

Bubble Trouble

Page 54
Cross-Outs

~~soccer~~	~~scarlet~~	~~straight~~	~~cloudy~~	~~rain~~
~~weight~~	~~baseball~~	no	~~turquoise~~	like
~~jet~~	~~gate~~	~~aqua~~	~~purple~~	~~tennis~~
~~sunny~~	there's	place	~~bluebird~~	home

Field Day Fun

First: Yasmin **Second:** Barb
Third: Sydney **Fourth:** Jill

Page 55
Letter Finish

1. Golf
2. Bowling
3. Tennis
4. Hockey
5. Gymnastics
6. Football

AG Code 3

He went to the game!

Pages 56, 57
Tricky Type

1. Grown up
2. A little fight between friends
3. Ring around the rosie
4. Doughnuts
5. Batter up
6. Forever
7. Fat chance
8. Up and at 'em
9. Hang out
10. Merry-go-round
11. Movie stars
12. Last straw
13. Buckle up
14. Crosswords
15. One thing after another
16. High five
17. A drop in temperature
18. Flat tire

Pages 58, 59

Fairy Tale Wordsearch

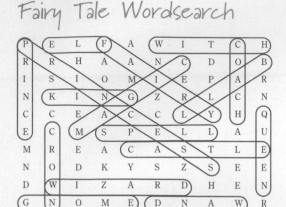

Twisted Tales

1. The Three Little Pigs
2. The Old Woman Who Lived in a Shoe
3. Sleeping Beauty
4. The Tortoise and the Hare
5. The Ugly Duckling
6. The Emperor's New Clothes
7. The Cat in the Hat
8. The Princess and the Pea

Page 60

Recess!

Possible answers:

sun, swing, squirrel, spider, snail, slide, sneakers, soccer ball, seesaw, sidewalk, stilts, snake, skateboard, sandbox, stairs, straw hat, string, stegosaurus, sack

Pages 62, 63

After-School Crossword

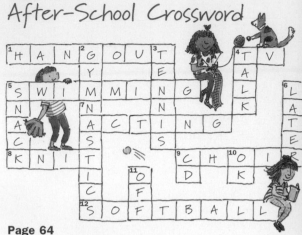

Page 64

To the Pet Shop!

Her puppy's name is SCOUT.

Page 65
Scrambled Doggies

1. dalmatian
2. beagle
3. boxer
4. poodle
5. husky
6. terrier
7. spaniel
8. retriever

Page 67
Crazy Coin Trick

1. Turn over coins 3 and 4.
2. Turn over coins 4 and 5.
3. Turn over coins 2 and 3.

Dimes to Pennies

Possible answer:

1 to 5

3 to 7 to 1

8 to 4 to 3 to 7

6 to 2 to 8 to 4 to 3

5 to 6 to 2 to 8

1 to 5 to 6

7 to 1

Page 69
AG Code 4

Because then it would be a foot!

Page 70
Cross-Outs

~~cat~~	~~lip~~	~~gardener~~	of	~~fabulous~~
a	~~lawyer~~	~~pill~~	~~angry~~	~~author~~
~~teacher~~	~~busy~~	~~pony~~	~~lively~~	~~raccoon~~
~~prickly~~	deck	~~Amy~~	cards	~~Erin~~

Twin Test

Page 72
Quick Dip Maze

Page 73
Seaside Scramble

1. seagull
2. crab
3. eel
4. octopus
5. seaweed
6. whale
7. starfish
8. shark

Pages 76, 77
Sweet Tooth Crossword

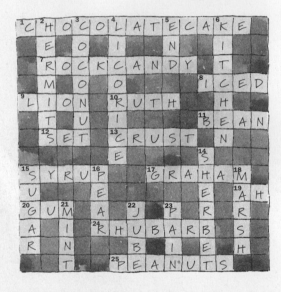

Pages 78, 79
Toothpick Tricks

1. Remove toothpicks A, B, and C.
2. Remove toothpicks C, E, and F.
3. Remove toothpicks B, E, H, and K.
4. Remove toothpicks D, F, G, and I.
5. Remove toothpicks F, G, J, and K.
6. Move toothpicks E, H, and G, so your fish looks like this:

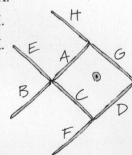

Page 80
Brainbenders

1. They all do.
2. New Year's Day and Christmas always fall in the same year.
3. In the dictionary.
4. Neither—16 + 9 = **25.**
5. One thousand nine hundred ninety-three pennies are worth $19.93—almost twenty dollars.
6. They are equal—a pound is a pound.
7. "Mispelled" should be "misspelled."
8. The other coin is a nickel! She has a quarter and a nickel.